This book belongs to

. . . .

For Little D—S.H.

OXFORD
UNIVERSITY PRESS

Oxford is a registered trademark
of Oxford University Press in the UK
and certain other countries

Text © Oxford University Press 2023
Illustrations © Sarah Horne 2023

All rights reserved.

British Library Cataloguing
in Publication Data

Data available

ISBN: 978-0-19-278655-5

Printed in China

www.oup.com

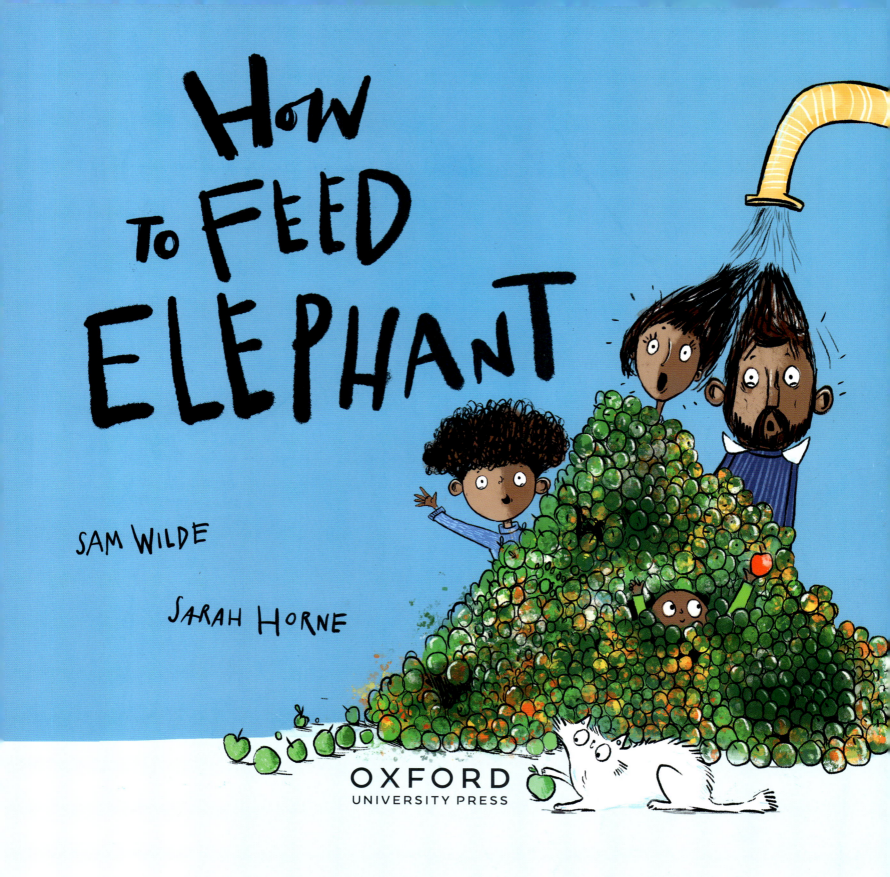

How to FEED ELEPHANT

SAM WILDE

SARAH HORNE

OXFORD
UNIVERSITY PRESS

Dad thinks we could get a puppy.

Mum thinks we could get a goldfish.

But I want an . . . .

You must make
sure a pet has
enough to eat.

It turns out, my elephant
eats quite a lot.

A pet should have
enough to drink.

It can't be *that* hard to find 200 litres a day.

Sometimes you have to wash your pet . . .

... though elephants prefer
taking mud baths.
Actually, I think I do too!

**That's because
his poo is . . .**

**. . . full of
seeds!**

Pets should have somewhere
comfortable to sleep.

the neighbours might not get much sleep either.

We're not sure this is actually the best place for my elephant to live.

I love my elephant and he loves me.

But we both think he'd be happier back home with his family.

I wonder who will come to stay next!

Top elephant facts!

There are three species of elephant: African Savanna, African Forest, and Asian.

The African Savanna elephant is the world's heaviest land animal. Adult males can weigh up to 7,500kg—that's about the same as 1,500 cats!

Wild elephants can live for 60–70 years.

Elephants can be right- or left-tusked, just like we can be right- or left-handed.

Elephants make their own sunscreen by taking dust and mud baths.

An elephant's trunk is so sensitive it can pick up a single grain of rice.

Elephants spend 12–18 hours a day eating.

Elephants eat grasses, shrubs, fruit, shoots, and roots, and eat up to 150kg of food a day—that's about the same as 1,000 apples!

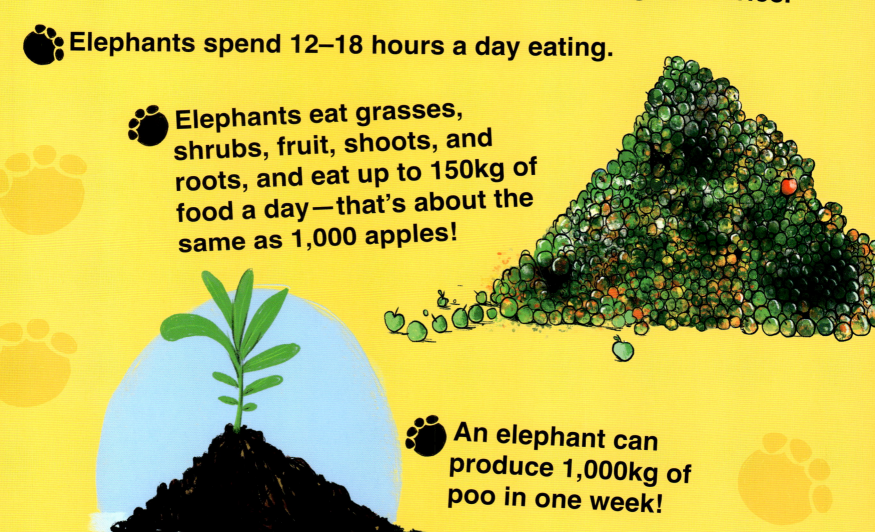

An elephant can produce 1,000kg of poo in one week!

Due to poaching for ivory and loss of habitat, around 90% of African elephants have been wiped out in the last century. Charities like the WWF work hard to protect endangered animals like elephants.
Find out more at their website: www.wwf.org.uk